One River

One River

Steve Armstrong

PUNCHER & WATTMANN

First published in 2023
Published by Puncher and Wattmann
PO Box 279
Waratah NSW 2298

https://www.puncherandwattmann.com
web@puncherandwattmann.com

ISBN   9781922571984

Cover design by Miranda Douglas
Back cover image: *Australia East coast New South Wales 1871 Hunter River surveyed by J.T.Gowlland assisted by J.F. Loxton (Courtesy of the National Library of Australia)*.
Edited by Ed Wright
Typesetting by Morgan Arnett
Printed by Lightning Source International

NATIONAL LIBRARY OF AUSTRALIA

A catalogue record for this work is available from the National Library of Australia

This collection is indebted to the child I was, who spent his every spare moment wandering among the angophoras and Hawkesbury sandstone, the country in West Turramurra that grew me up. I'm almost certain that poetry would not have found me, if my mother—Marion—had not shared my love of wilder places where one could find solitude, and allowed me to venture far and often.

Contents

Beginnings[1]

This book began with a poem about an island. Ash Island[2] lies in the Hunter River estuary, and its westernmost point—blunt as the prow of a barge—shoulders the river into a north and a south arm. It's a place I go for replenishment, to be among the water birds that frequent its wetlands, and to marvel at raptors like the swamp harriers as they patrol the marshes and reed banks. At first I imagined this island piece would remain a stand-alone poem, but when my friend Paul McNamara[3] read a draft version he was enthused, and suggested I might travel the watershed of the Hunter and write a series of such works. I needed no convincing that the poem, like the island, was part of something larger; his idea became my own. And so it was in the first year of the pandemic—between lock-downs—I set out to know the river better.

The poems that constitute this book are meditations on the Hunter River written as haibun, a Japanese poetic form made up of prose punctuated by haiku. The best known haibun is Basho's (1644–94) *The Narrow Road to the Deep North*[4]. A work that records his peregrinations in the last decade of his life, the haiku in it are linked snapshots of the landscape and his state of mind as he travelled. In this collection of haibun, Korean sijo replace the haiku, and while the sijo is, like the haiku brief, it's a longer form which allowed me the room to make a substantial lyric response to the birds, the trees and the weather I encountered on the river. In my mind, the sijo in their relative compression are analogous to a river rapids—or the quick-step that's the banter of a brook—and on the other hand, the prose in its amplitude has more in common with the wider, calmer reaches of a stream.

I've not made a survey of the river catchment; I've been far less orderly. I've rambled along its course, immersed myself in the labyrinthine network that is its tributaries: the Allyn; the Paterson; the Chichester;

the Williams; the Carrowbrook; and Massey's Creek, to name a few. On a whim I followed back roads through hills and valleys, and when it seemed they might peter out, continued on in hope they would widen again, and carry me to another branch of the river's venous network. I could say, as Aldo Leopold[5] did, in the subtitle to his *A Sand County Almanac*, I've made sketches here and there.

I wasn't inclined to track down the Hunter's headwaters, or to visit the river's every capillary. I resisted the narrative imperative to write the river from beginning to end, and followed the lyric impulse instead, which Gregory Orr explains, in his *A Primer for Poets and Readers of Poetry*[6], generates a poem that "constellates around a single center such as a dominant feeling...or situation." I also harboured a notion that walking with the river would align with a perennial feeling I have, that the process of imagining and writing poetry itself, takes the form of a river, one which belongs to the geography of my interior. Frederic Gros[7] insists walking has a way of "prising us from the obsession with doing," and that it "puts us in touch with that childhood eternity once again." Going to the river has been like that.

Water constitutes much of our body—is elemental to our physiology—which may explain why we find rivers, lakes and oceans entrancing. Further on this subject, Gaston Bachelard[8] suggests that reverie possesses the logic of water, that our imaginations depend on a fluid relationship between sense and imagery; a fluvial chemistry. When I surrender to the river and its hinterland, when I quieten the masculine ways of being as they're formulated in my culture, when I devote as much of my awareness as possible to what's around me, then unusual— at times improbable—leaps of imagination and dream-like stretches of waking consciousness come over me. These happenings lie at the heart of this collection; I believe in their whimsical complexity, and that they constitute overlooked truths, truths distinct from those that arise from objective observations of a river. Barry Lopez[9] writes of the manner in which indigenous peoples maintain a "continuous attentiveness to both the obvious (scientific) and ineffable(artistic)orders of the local landscape." This understanding marries poet John Burnside's assertion—in *Strong Words: modern poets on modern poetry*[10]—that "...a reasoned, functional view of the world is vital" but it must be "...moderated by the spiritual..." that is, "...a way of thinking both reverent and inventive in its vision of nature..." I set out with the intention that such a vision would animate the haibun in this collection; I hope you find it so.

Hunter-gatherer cultures, according to Charles Foster in his book *Being Human: Adventures in Forty Thousand Years of Consciousness*[11], like Australian indigenous peoples—who I'd point out have been around much longer than forty thousand years—view all of creation, all matter, as alive and "ensouled", and therefore inclined toward congress with human beings. Well inland of the city of Newcastle, New South Wales, where I live, is an aboriginal sacred site known as "The Northern Map Site". It's a rock platform on a ridge line close to Mt Yengo—a mountain of great significance to indigenous peoples of the east coast of Australia, in most part because the Dreamtime creator-being Biami, stepped down from the sky here and left the mountain with its distinctive flattened profile. An Aboriginal elder with detailed knowledge of sacred sites in the area[12] explained that the figures and animals etched in this sandstone shelf were designed to instruct people—who once gathered here in large numbers for extended ceremony—in the lore they needed to be mindful of. One group of human-like beings cut into the stone, have rays radiating from their heads toward the sky, while around their waists are belts that slant down sharply to signify connection to the earth. Most striking are their enormous round eyes and the absence of a mouth. I was told this was a directive something like—"Open your eyes, and be quiet..."—because immersion in the Dreaming[13] can't happen if one is constantly talking.

One morning recently I was out walking before sun up. The sky was chalky-blue, and the clouds banked above the horizon wore a diaphanous robe of pink. Naturally enough, I sought words for this loveliness, but only when I abandoned my efforts to capture this fleeting beauty with language, did embodied feelings germinate within me. Quickly a felt-sense permeated me, a lightness of being anchored to the earth and nurturing as a homecoming. I could have wept. Was this a spiritual encounter, did I for those few moments experience the sparks of my own divinity[14]? Perhaps it's a matter of my soul having more living room, space to breath? Then again it might be that awareness which is available when we transcend language and the worried workings of our intellect, "when the whole body is one sense and imbibes delight through every pore[15]". I believe this is what Seamus Heaney is getting at when he speaks of making a "...raid on the inarticulate...[16]", which in his view is what poetic apprehension depends on. I speak of this a little in a poem of mine, "On the Delta[17]"

> "...this solid thing that's light within you—
> let it wing into the regions of wider
> sight, let it feel for the company of words."

What I'm proposing, in large part anyway, is that our everyday use of language diminishes our ability to experience the richness of the world around us, and that in particular falls short of evoking the "joyous ache"[18] we feel before a sunrise, a river, or a tree. You might be thinking wait a minute, this book of poems is comprised of words, and sentences, and therefore depends on the very system whose reductive qualities you're calling into question. My answer would be this: as I see it, poetry has always been an attempt to craft words in such a way they transcend the utilitarian use of language; Buson, painter and haiku poet said "... use the commonplace to escape the commonplace[19]".

Poetic endeavour to re-imagine the quotidian relies heavily on metaphor, and as Ian McGilchrist[20] writes in his book *The Master and his Emissary*—an exploration of how the two hemispheres of the human brain influence behaviour and culture—"The point of a metaphor is to bring together the whole of one thing with the whole of another, so that each is looked at in a different light." He also suggests "...metaphor asserts a common life that is experienced in the body of the one who makes it, and the separation is only present at the linguistic level." This final thought aligns squarely with the notion, that the sense of coherence which is a poetic impulse, is born of embodied consciousness. Consistent with this understanding, I can attest to how at times I felt "a common life" with the river, a nascent sense of my animal capacity for flow as manifested in the limber movements of the river.

Seamus Heaney[21], contemplating the protracted civil war that afflicted his home country of Ireland, writes of how he found himself unable to resist the conclusion that "...history is about as instructive as an abattoir...". However, he then goes on to describe his efforts to arrive at a poetic response to his country's war-torn strife, and how this led him to try and make space in his "...reckoning and imagining for the marvellous as well as the murderous." As the descendant of an invader culture that murdered and raped the first peoples of this country, that systematically stole their land and degraded their culture, I find Heaney's words particularly telling. They offer me a framework within which, on the one hand, I might continue to be conscious of the terrible inter-generational cost of invasion for the first peoples of this continent, and on the other hand, might dare to foster an ecstatic relationship to this land, its animals and forms.

In my approach to the river I've invited those aspects of myself that still reverberate with my roots in nature—those that cannot live without wild things[22]—to freely express themselves. And yet, I acknowledge that my translation of this raw material is not straightforward, it will inevitably reflect to some degree, my age, my class, my gender, my family and cultural background, as well as the landscapes I grew up in, which is not to mention my particular loves and hates, my privilege and disadvantage, as well as my experiences of grief and of illness. Mark Tredinnick[23] in his *The Land's Wild Music,* suggests that despite our suppositions, we might nevertheless try and let ourselves be surprised by our encounters with the other than human world. I hope this collection transmits some of the calm and exhilaration, the vulnerability and potency I experienced in the river's embrace. It is also my wish—to paraphrase Tredinnick[24] from another of his essays—that this book of poems will further your desire to include rivers, mountains and forests in the story of who you are, that your sense of yourself as a human might encompass more than the digital and the social dimensions of your life, will be informed by other than human places and their resident beings.

If love is the genesis of art—a painting, a drawing or a poem—then art-making, like falling in love, is an encounter that heightens one's sense of self, and simultaneously entails its loss. Herein lies beauty. John Berger[25], writing of Van Gogh's art, ventures that his works are essentially acts of love and gratitude. Berger wonders out loud whether the gratitude we feel in the presence of a painting by Van Gogh, belongs to the place (the subject), the artist or to the viewer? I'm not sure I can answer this question, but may you the reader as you move through this collection, have a sense of the gratitude I felt travelling the catchment, and find a poem or a passage or two, that call you "back from the realm of the merely factual to the mystery of the real[26]". In turn, may these poems encourage you to defend the real thing that's a river as one of your own.

Ash Island

"Intervals of dreaming help us stand up under days of work."
—Pablo Neruda, from his *Memoirs*.

An island[27] ghosted by mangrove and the forked tidal channels of a river delta; much of it mud and wetland, low-lying and inclined to flood. To get there, cross a narrow concrete span over the southernmost branch of the river, where from the height of the bridge you can see into a sepia gallery—the broad reach of mangrove to the east—and for that moment, you're outside the flow of time. You arrive and pull up. Imagine for a moment, that stepping on the island is setting foot on a vessel, one that rides a great confluence to its end.

On the island, the system of thought that organises my calendar, the one that compiles, then ticks off tasks on my to-do-lists—for that's its greatest satisfaction—is the mind I want to walk away from. Left unopposed, this inner Descartes always gets ahead of himself, a colonising evangelist, he mistrusts the mystery that's a mangrove. I go to the island for the birds, and to borrow—for a while—the fluidity that's the mind of trees, and of water. I go for breadth of being, and to breathe, rather than gasp.

> The she-oaks by the river
> are slow dancing; all the brides
> of a briny nor'easter.
> Wanderers[28]—burnt-sienna
> angels—laugh at gravity;
> what fidelity to faithless air.

In the 1860s the island was cleared of rain forest and its wetlands drained for dairy farming. Most of the blueberry ash trees—after which white settlers named the place—had already been felled for a fine-grained timber both light and strong, fit for the ribs of a boat. In my explorations of the island, I've found but one mature ash.

Today the island is a wild place coming back to itself and yet it endures ongoing human impositions; high tension power lines march through the middle of the wetlands and carry electricity across the water to the industrial precincts beyond the river's northern bank.

> I find the island's schoolhouse;
>> a ruin crowned in blackberry.
> A persimmon prospers, bright
>> over broken stone walls. High
> wire pylons take giant steps;
>> a bird plays the treble oboe.

There are other ruins: a wartime radar station, a concrete igloo beside footings that once supported an aerial, but there's no trace of the barracks that housed its crew—one for women, and one for men. To the east, a close-knit stand of northern hemisphere pines. Their sombre green gives way to frost-burned pasture, and under my feet the yellowed grasses release a scent with a heart-note that speaks of all this island was.

> On a potholed road, a mud
>> lark and the rasp of dry rushes.
> I scare a pair of buff-banded
>> rail—their chicks remain well hidden.
> Rocks in the river shallows.
>> A butcher bird's morning chorus.

I cross the mangrove, not on a boardwalk, but where the water—like clear resin—flows over mud between iron-clad trunks. It's hard to say if the tide is coming in, or going out. I study the play of light in the tiny whirlpools that form behind the trunks of these amphibious trees, and catch a fish in the outer reaches of my vision. Who am I in this place that's neither land nor river, light nor dark?

> A path knee-high with grass, I
>   almost step on a red-belly
> that dreams of frogs—a sudden
>   flick and she's gone. A butterfly
> enjambs her lines, brushes my
>   arm to remind me I'm in luck.

Early one morning not long ago, I walked the island when the light was the first wash on cotton rag, and clouds swarmed like jelly-fish on the ebb tide, grey and darker grey, then steeped in gold. How can I feel such melancholy when the dawn is so? A busy school of mullet pass close to the bank. One iridescent flash after another—the fish lift my mood. I track a dorsal shimmer through the skies behind my heart, tuck crooked wings and plummet.

With winter behind us the weather is warming, and it won't be long before swarms of Hexham-grey mosquitoes[29] trail me where ever I go. I fear their vampirish bite, and the aches and pains it can bring. Now is the time for walking.

> Over the river's north arm
>   in the shadow of the mangrove,
> an egret stationed on one
>   leg meditates on the tide, waits
> for the flats to be shallows.
>   Way up, ravens joust.

Soon I'll drive home, pull a coffee short, and sit down to hammer away at the anvil, my desk, to beat and stretch what glows. I'll pretend I'm forging Damascus steel folding it over and over till it fuses. It's a medieval recipe for the keenest edge—a metallurgy lost to modern smiths—steel with a patterned face that mimics flowing water. I'll cut and polish and pray for water's mark.

A River Within Reach

On the upper Chichester, under a low bridge, the river runs in easy strides over polished stones of green and tan, black and deepest brown. Gazing down into this clear current—drawn to it as if my body were a dowsing rod—a tingling begins in the soles of my feet, and it migrates through me, a correspondence unmuddied by thought, between the unbound stream beneath me and my watery constitution. I've a longing to be lost in the river, to become another arm of its being. This river, not far from its source in the Barringtons— which command the skyline to the northwest—is on the one hand a distillation of place and, on the other hand, it's ceaseless movement an exquisite embodiment of life as unending pilgrimage.

For some years I've imagined poetry's beginnings as a river—the stream of books I read, and the currents running beneath the lines I make. More than a metaphor, this sense of poetry as a river is a matter of trusting the whole-of-being sense that prefigures thought, a felt sense for those numinous threads of knowing that poets hope they might translate for the page.

I remember a time, when the 737 carrying me home surfed a turbulent cumulonimbus like a kayak pitched about by whitewater. My face pressed to the window, I got to thinking about how a river begins, and where it ends.

> Rain beats a rivered tempo
>   on my roof. Any body of
> water has many mothers.
>   If we count me and you as part
> of this infinity—why
>   then, do we only claim the one?

In spring and summer, a nor'easter blows in off the south arm of the river. When it arrives I open my windows so that it might grace my home. The breeze is a lover of salty exhalations, of the egret's slow high-step on the mud flats at low tide, and of the ruined scent of axle grease thick on the tracks that guide cargo-weary cranes from ship to ship. It freshens my day.

The footings of my house are brick piers. There are forty-two of them not counting those beneath the back deck. They stand on alluvial deposits forsworn by the river; deep and loamy, this soil once lay beneath native grasslands and islands of she-oaks. Country managed lightly, sung into being by the Awabakal[50]—where, for an inconceivably long time, they fattened kangaroos and tended fields of yam daisy[31]. I picture a vast patchwork in flower, a flux of yellow—a dying constellation's evanescent burst of colour.

On the flats by the river, on this plumb-bob level land— with a branch line nearby—Broken Hill Propriety Ltd (BHP)opened a steelworks in 1915. What a complex: coke ovens, two blast furnaces dispensing fiery streams and plumes of ash, and a slab-sided roll shop which could house a jumbo jet. Today the admin building stands unused and circled by chain-lock fencing; in soviet style, it still gives nothing away.

Eighty years of steel-making
    by the river—molten ingots
three shifts a day. A black talc
    settled in each roof's void—it slips
through my ceiling boards. Caulk them
    with No More Gaps; it's gone away.

Back then, fly-ash turned clean
    washing black, and smouldered in workers'
lungs too—their deaths foretold
    by coal. My neighbour, a foundry-man,
was taken to hospital
    last Monday—he'll never come home.

This neighbour of mine told me of how he drilled down for the water table, that his bore spike pulled clean and clear at nine metres. The avocado tree in my yard—of the Shepard variety—must draw water from way down too, because it supports a spreading crown, and most years bears a healthy crop in March and April. Seamus Heaney[32] writes that poetry is the work of divination, of getting "in touch with what is there, hidden and real," of "going outside of normal cognitive bounds", to "raid the inarticulate". Informed by him, I sometimes picture poetry's beginnings in the sweet water that percolates into a well, that I'm dipping into the cool darkness of an underground reservoir.

According to the French philosopher Gaston Bachelard[33] the English word *riv-er* has "a sonorous brutality" a masculine tone and rhythm that lacks the ability to communicate the nature of water flowing. The French word for a river that runs to the sea is *riv-i-e-re*— four syllables and a feminine noun of imagination that flows as you speak it, that resonates in your chest, and then skips lightly off the tip of your tongue. A word with vulnerability and power.

I came across an aerial photograph of BHP when it was running at full tilt in the 1960s. It looks like a city under bombardment, a battlefield shrouded in swirling clouds of dark smoke, punctured here and there by tall columns of steam pumped from chimney stacks. The earth around it is an aching wound. It speaks of a certain kind of masculinity—and I'm thinking here of the institution, not the working people who held jobs there—that cluster of attitudes and habits that inform a man who perpetrates domestic violence, who's indifferent to the pain he inflicts on his loved ones in pursuit of his needs, and when an attempt is made to hold him to account, will deny responsibility for the damage his actions and neglect have caused. In fact, he believes that in being confronted, he's the victim.

> Chlorides for pickling steel, slag
>   of lead, mercury and manganese
> were a few of the toxic
>   metals bound for the bottom, and
> its dwellers. I'll still eat
>   the river's prawns; they taste so sweet.

For several decades after the closure of the steel plant, the site remained an unremediated wasteland[34]. I went there often, ignoring the signs that warned of contamination, and wandered around like the kid I once was, charmed by broken bits of machinery, abandoned buildings, wattles groves and pampas grass. I found solitude there, it was the kind of place I could set aside worries, and more.

> Gutted cars and the empty
>   buildings in this forgotten
> lot by the river. I go
>   there to cauterize my sorrows;
> there's comfort in the company
>   of the soiled and the ruined.

When I reflect on the river and the breadth of its catchment, I can't escape the thought that my life—and the scope of my writing—would be better for travelling more widely than I do. I think of the revered haiku poet Basho who gave up his house and his possessions to wander northern Japan in the last ten years of his life. When I seek guidance on this matter from that deeper part of me that inspires poetry, ask it whether I should take to the road or not, it naturally enough answers on the side of Basho. A river's course is a mind made up by water's motion and the terrain it passes through; and life is something like that. I might stay put in a quiet backwater, but all the while the source that set me moving urges me on, says run from this lie, lean into the bend before me.

Rivers of the Mind

On the upper Allyn, between Lady's Well and Lagoon Pinch Forest Road, a leviathan rock turns the current—a loping flow—through a narrows and into a rapids. At the end of the race, the stream's rushing dilates in a still sparkling, almond-eyed pool. There's a vigour with which the river is quiet here, a trace of the ineffable which draws me into the nested shade of trees arching out from the bank.

> Frogs croak low down like hinges
>   on a crooked door. A fantail takes
> it higher, while the river's
>   lyric is of nothing if not
> contentedness. A pair
>   of wood ducks rifle by on purpose.

A river is memory in motion. Today, beguiled by the Allyn's flow, I remember a boulder-strewn reach of the Gloucester, where after stretching out on my stomach, and settling down into the river's rocky bed—as if to purge my mind of thought—a superb lyrebird stepped from the forest and leapt onto a podium mid-stream. The bird must have mistaken me for a lump of granite, because it dropped its tail below half-mast, and flapping it wings wildly, leapt in and out of the water performing a manic bathing ritual.

> Glassy, the river is clear
>   sky made liquid. I'm eye to eye
> with the river's duende;
>   it has no fear of falling. The rocks
> beneath me finger my flesh
>   and sinew; they sound for my depths.

Water freshens former beauties—as when you pluck a polished cobble from a dry stream bed and wet it, or as Gaston Bachelard puts it "The sight of a stream reawakens distant dreams...[55]". On my way home from the river—driving as if the road itself were fluvial—I'm lost to reverie, back at Blue Hole on the Gara River, camped with my girlfriend in a small grassy square which opens on a garden of speckled igneous boulders. The edge of gorge country. She shucks off her jeans, a tear above the knee, leg seams stitched with yellow thread faded with wear, and now her bikini bottom tied at the hip. Across time, she looks at me through long sun-burned bangs, the freckles on her cheeks, and the tender light from her green eyes, a distant nebula.

> A sleeping bag unzipped, tartan
>   lining turned up with knowledge
> of the night. We pack our gear,
>   and then ford the river below
> the welded lip that's water
>   over a weir; it's perfectly clear.

Up until I was eight years of age, my family lived on the edge of a bush land valley reserve in West Turramurra, a three-quarter acre block of land contiguous with Lane Cove National Park, if you overlook the interruption of the Comenarra Parkway which lay between. Water Dragon Creek ran along the bottom of the valley, and the Eastern Water Dragons who gave the stream its name, would sun themselves on every other snag and boulder. Me and my best friend Ian—who almost always had a lizard dangling from a pocket, reptiles who seemed to enjoy his company as much as I did—hero worshipped the Aboriginal people, the Kuringai who had been evicted from the bush we roamed. I cannot say for sure how they came to be central to our imaginings. I do know my mother spoke of them, shared something of what she'd read of the first peoples. I noticed her respect and detected sorrow. Perhaps it was what we perceived as their freedom from what trapped us, school and the rest of it. Ian, I recall, feared the school bus like a species of death.

> Refuse one last confinement—
>   a seat on the school bus—race down
> the hill instead. The work of
>   our play—ancestors, not by blood
> but ours by love of place. We
>   imagined ourselves ancient.

Unschooled in the real effects of invasion—and too young to question where we belonged—me and Ian felt a tangible fellowship with the black figures we felt moving through the angophoras and Hawkesbury sandstone, much more than we did with our teachers and classmates. Reflecting on the implacable nature of our resistance to school, I've come to the conclusion that in the inchoate manner of two small boys, we intuited where our culture was threadbare; in a reflex way, we wanted our schooling to be as alive as the rocks and red gums, as gnarled as the old man banksias and water dragons. And so it was we coveted indigenous technologies of hand and eye, longed to fashion spears and tools from the materials at hand, objects born of an intimate engagement with this country that cradled us.

These rememberings—though at times elusive in translation—belong to the perennial stream that was our ceaseless play, to the grammar of the sandstone that we learned with our hands and knees—the grip its coarse grain granted our sneakered feet, or how much bounce the deeply scented leaf litter between the fissures in the standing boulders, offered skin and bone when we slipped and fell. These things were the bedrock of our being, of a self-possession we felt nowhere but in this bushland.

Everyday a wound. Our blood
        was spilt on sandstone and fallen
leaves. The bull ants bit us, bush
        ticks loved the warmth of our skin.
Our minds, our flesh, infected so
        as to bear the spirit of place.

Jerusalem Creek is a tributary of the Chichester River in the upper reaches of the Hunter catchment. I walk the slopes above the stream enjoying the easy-going company of old-growth tallowwoods. Beside them, blue-gums glow in the filtered light, their unblemished trunks lean, creamy, and tinted green. I feel no need to overstate my appreciation, silence and a nod in their direction is enough; above, a dark canopy flickers and dances with starbursts of light. I've not seen my childhood friend Ian in five decades, but today I imagine he's walking with me.

Unnamed, I'd call it "Little
        Song" or "Delicate", a solo
partita scored in the boy
        soprano range—a brook unbrooked
until it joins the sudden
        main—lost in the nature of things.

Philosopher-architect Christopher Alexander[36], writes of a "pattern language" common to wilderness, and to the buildings whose spaces we feel most alive and at home in. Alexander says we're attuned to more than beauty here, we discern a "goodness" when a place built or wild, is "true to its own inner forces..." and not because it displays any "... special sense of purpose." Human relationships possess a pattern language also. My friendship with Ian struck a fundamental note in me, and the soulful connections I've experienced as adult share the same tonality; they encompass an embodied love of being in the bush, an understanding felt and not necessarily spoken, that to grow up a part of nature, means certain aspects of self depend upon a reverent attention to a wild place for their recovery and expression. The final lines of Mary Oliver's poem *Wild Geese*[37] sing of such a notion.

> ...the world offers itself to your imagination,
> calls to you like the wild geese, harsh and exciting—
> over and over announcing your place
> in the family of things.

I descend to the edge of the stepped rock chute that carries the creek; the water and autumn light race each other down one precipitous cascade after another. At my feet is a small channel, a short-lived diversion from the main current. I crouch down low for this slight anabranch, for the slant strata and the weathered face of its bed. It's the mother-creek in miniature.

> A creek bed of well-worn stone
>> bares a tessellated grin.
> Water, a deft mimic, dances
>> the light to mirror the rock,
> makes a pulsing and tiled
>> array. Here then, is truth in play.

The Real World[38] is Song

Up the road from Old Camp, I edge in against a wall of forest and cut the engine. There's a half-hidden track to the river here—damp soil, outcroppings of rock, and a spare under-storey of shrubs beneath native laurel and skyward oaks. Beyond the steepling shade of the trees, the light lives at the river's pace—and my gaze won't hold either; it's swept downstream. I crouch on a watermarked stone, and hope its natural reticence[39] will steady me. As the water curves by the rock, it's so slick, so clear, I'd swear it's molten glass. The freshly enamelled stones that pave the water's course are vivid in a way Monet could not have captured.

> Look up the river oak—
>   a stag horn and bird's nest. At my feet
> a carpet of needles and
>   maidenhair ferns whose tiny dishes
> tilt the light. The river rocks
>   water and stone, a polyrhythmic
>
> jam of walking bass running,
>   while the butcher birds's song is all
> sweet sophistry. On the far bank
>   trees lean over the water. They're
> motionless in the still air;
>   as if about to take the stage.

Someone has made a city of miniature pebble pagodas at the water's edge. To find these structures in a wild place—no matter how small they maybe—angers me; I came here to escape the built environment. With venom I kick them down and rant as if the builders of these small cairns were here in front of me: "This is no Roman aqueduct, no place to scrawl *I too, was here*. You must kill such impulse, allow the still pool and the rose maple over the limpid water, the pale gold stones and shifting shadow, to inform instead." When I'm done raging, I see that I miss the point; these offerings, these tiny temples, created by balancing one small rock on top another, involve a kind of meditation that might well channel the river's flow. When I knock them down, they leave no trace; I'm still of the view it's more honourable to leave no obvious sign of our human presence.

> I cannot judge the passage
> > of time on the river, it runs—
> an undifferentiated
> > flow. But I've bills to pay
> and work this afternoon;
> > eventually I break the river's spell.

This summer has been wet and cool. Some scientists put it down to the polar ice caps melting; whatever the reason the rain has holed sections of the unsealed way through the valley, and my progress is erratic as I swerve and skid, dodging the potholes that the patterns of light and shadow on the surface of the dirt, disguise. Back on asphalt, the front suspension groans with each dip in the road; something has come undone.

The Dorribang[40] – The Williams

An old friend and I drive north on blue metal and bitumen for Dungog, then Salisbury, where the road narrows, crouches and takes the bends that are hill country, then opens and glides by milking sheds and river flats. At the foot of the Barringtons we leave the car. It's January, the height of summer and the heat of the day is building, so we welcome the shade of the back-lit blue gums, lime-washed pillars that hold the roof high. Their clerestory windows call on the sky to preach, but we pass on the sermon, and move on through the canopied shade stepping around looped vines. We're looking for the wreckage of rocks that's the Williams in its upper reaches.

Offline for the Dorribang,
    its untrammelled flow. On the brink
of a fall, bright waters
    from the Tops pause, play the moment
without a sign of motion.
    Touch the flank of a flooded-gum.

Tumbled granite with the weight of a mountain: we find a seat and cleave to the sounds of the stream before us, a riffle that runs short and fast and into a pool; its mouth a sculpted chute of stone. Opposite is a rock whose Neanderthal brow hides an unwavering gaze. When I point it out, my friend decides it's not a vengeful water-spirit, but a gnome wearing a brown felt hat. He tells me he's going in search of an eel where the water loses its way over a pebble bottom, and the wide reaching branches of a river-oak—that's read all three volumes of The Lord of the Rings—create a patchwork of light and dark.

As a boy in New Zealand
    you'd tramp far in the rain
to set lines in a brook. Hungry,
    you'd smoke your catch over
green boughs of tea-tree brush—you
    were happy here, this your home.

The day will be a scorcher, but the sky remains icy-blue and unclouded. A wind blows lightly out of the north, and is freshened by its passage over the river. But every now and then, we're mugged by a warm mulled-wine body of air, still, dark and sweet with the odours of leaf litter rotting on the forest floor.

Stone by stone we run the river
    bed, each leap a heightened
moment, the broken ankle
    that might have been. In our steps
a fear of falling and love
    of flight; we make like a rapids.

We stop by a tributary, a creek whose last moment is a waterfall, it throws a spume like a wave breaking before an offshore wind. Me and you, we've some catching up to do, and it stings me when I tell you how slow I've been to comprehend that intensity is no measure of love, and that ease with the ordinary is an under-appreciated type of beauty. I'm reminded, how with tact, you spoke to me of this matter years ago. I also recall I was deaf to your efforts to wake me. Perhaps the nature of a good friendship is that we allow each other room to come and go, to fall, and then find our way again.

All rivers are inclined
    to dissolution. Mythic while

muddy, some grow deltas and
　　others bifurcate for a north
and a south arm—their final
　　confluence an act of friendship.

Upstream slabs of tilted strata jut into the path of the river. We decide to see what's on the other side; my friend is still on the hunt for an eel, short-finned or long, it doesn't matter. He speaks of their life cycle, how after maybe thirty years the eels leave the pools that are their home, for breeding grounds in the Coral Sea. They cover thousands of sea miles, and all the while they're dying.

In the manner of the stream
　　it lives in, an eel is quick
and slow. Like water, it carries
　　a memory of where it came from
and where it's going; back in
　　the ocean, all it hears is home.

Our return journey unfolds like the easy reach of a river, and the car's motion goes with it. Together we marvel at the story of baby eels. Glass eels they're called at first—filaments of light almost undetectable in water—and then, when they grow opaque, they're elvers. The uncanny bit, is how they find their way back to the stream where their ancestors lived; nobody can quite explain it.

Evening light and jersey cows;
　　languid they cross the road udders
groaning. Idling there a while,
　　we settle for the rhythms
and smells, and we smile
　　at the farmer's curt nod to move off.

Short of Dungog we take a poorly patched side road, a detour across the river and then along its eastern bank. Friends of mine used to live near here, and my memories are fond. We stop and walk the streaming pebble bed. I pick a few polished stones and work them like worry beads.

> The low deck of a timber
>   bridge over the cobble bed
> of the Williams. She-oaks mid-
>   stream, and the tang of a rounded
> pebble in my mouth. It
>   tells me of everywhere it's been.

Wanderings

On Farmhouse Way the land I'm crossing lies "flat as slumber[41]", meadows cleared of rain forest for grazing in the back half of the nineteenth century. Once more I'm walking Ash Island. For the last decade or more, this island in the river has been undergoing remediation[42]: rows of seedling stock have been planted to regenerate the forest communities it was once blanketed with, and sections of mangrove uprooted, so that the salt marshes upon which migratory shorebirds depend for foraging, might recover. I approach the ruins of a school house, and stop to snap a shot of fallen blocks of sandstone and an ageing persimmon's elegant bones. I try several times, but fail to frame this scene's Wabi-sabi[43] accent.

A Japanese sensibility, Wabi-sabi began to take shape in the 15th century as a slant take on the traditional tea ceremony. It means among a great many other things, to find beauty in the "irregular", or "at the edge of nothingness", "to be desolate" and to take "pleasure in that which is old, faded, and lonely...".

Once school children paraded
    now a blackberry thicket. Their
dairies on the estuary,
    wiped out in the fifty-five
flood, a lesson of course, but
    not one found in the syllabus.

Before I turn toward the track that will take me along the northern arm of the river, I stop for the open country around me—three times I make a slow sweep from left to right. I want to know if I'm alone. And it's not only the scrutiny of others I seek freedom from, but that entity within me—who made camp long ago—that calls up shame at will. I discovered at a young age that one of the few times I could be myself—could escape my fear of being judged inadequate—was to be immersed in nature. In the first place I found this peace in the red-gum and sandstone country around my family's first home in West Turramurra. I spent as much time as I could in this bush land; the only true antidote to the oppression I experienced at school.

Another part of my inspiration for engaging with country in a studied manner, are the observations[44] Barry Lopez makes of an Eskimo hunter who conducts a long and painstaking audit of the tundra with a borrowed pair of binoculars. Lopez's point, it seems to me, is that proper attention to country is an intricate process that takes as long as it takes, and that when one shows such particular care, it's a form of respect, if not compassion, for one's self, as well as the land.

In my case, I'm not sure if the finer points of this place find me or if I find them. A nearby copse of swamp oaks, their trunks a dark and cabled yarn, are warp to the weft the spiders have woven—a net to catch the morning sun. A low branching and blackened gum beside me is creamy with flowers, and whispers to a slight sou-sou-westerly. Above, welcome swallows—like acrobatic pilots—scribble lines that only a man from the moon, such as Mr Squiggle, could figure.

River—a swollen tongue
    of dirty water. Frogs bleat thanks
for the floods of February,
    their estates grown. An egret flies
low, brilliant white
    before the mangrove's dark interior.

An osprey swings by, following the egret along the mangrove's towering edge on the far bank of this arm of the Hunter. Not knowing why I've an urge to look up—when I do a swamp harrier is hovering directly over me. We watch each other closely: her underbelly is downy, dappled fawn and rufous, and even if her unruffled gaze causes me to shiver—revives that fear I'm prey—I'm glad to be seen by her.

> A wetland pond. A reed bank
>   stirs. A hawk gauges the air, then
> falls twenty floors as if on
>   a wire. A black swan glances back
> at her greyish fleet. The hawk
>   meanders. But no kill today.

The sight of a monarch butterfly tilting in flight will always seduce my eye; their common name is better—the wanderer. I encounter these burnt-orange beauties on the island, but today I can find none. I'm surprised how hollow I feel without their jaunty jottings for company.

> A drowsiness nests within
>   me. I could curl up in it—so
> weary now with sorrow. But
>   when a swamp hen flashes me
> from the reeds—bares purple and red—
>   I crack a smile that clears my head.

My mind is a chainsaw. Even when it's only ticking over, it's primed to clear fell the old growth forest that's the present moment—its formula for the future is endless rows of pinus radiata. Today is no different, and full of hubris I hustle down an avenue of she-oaks. These trees are not giants, but tall and sculpted enough to cast shadows true to the nature of life barely above the water line. Chastened by them, I fall back in time with place, and each step becomes less about pushing off and more of a cyclical motion. Now I'm taller through the earth—as much of me below, as is above.

> Another eel's carcass at the
>   water's edge. The fishers who
> pulled them out don't love them.
>   My kiwi mate does. The wind picks
> up, saying something loudly.
>   Another eel slung in a dead tree.

It troubles me to weigh how humans degrade the land and its creatures. I'm reluctant to attend, in a clear-eyed way, to all that asks for recognition, to all that's been lost and damaged. When I do, I know what's being asked of me; perhaps that's why I drink.

> Tah-ib-ihn[45]—the river mouth.
>   Mu-lu-bin-ba—the meadows
> nearby. Watt-a-wan—the flat-
>   head, Wal-an-ga-ra—mullet, and
> Kul-go-nang—the kangaroo.
>   Brolgas gone from the tidal flats.

A magpie heavy through the middle, wings away from me at eye level, crosses open ground for a distant tree line. The harrier again: sliding sideways it misses nothing, and gathers speed over the dry rushes of a wetland. A pair of furiously fast parrots, I'm unable to identify, fly over in bounding flight. They're trumped by that pack of swallows, who pull crazy Gs as they climb, wings tucked tight—a perpendicular dash.

At last a wanderer,
    who beguiles with her dipping flight.
The eastern rosellas speed
    back the way they came, their markings
are unmistakable now;
    everything illuminated.

The Upper Allyn

A river is many things. One of them is water, another is a bard whose lyrics are a play on granite and sandstone. The Allyn becomes the Paterson, becomes the Hunter which is joined by the Williams, and this immensity is lost to the depths of the Tasman Sea. Today I take the Allyn River Road into the foothills of the Barringtons. As I drive I imagine the beginnings of a tributary in the ranges: a cloudburst finds a stretch of forest floor, where fallen rain drops feel for each other—they love to be a lively choir again.

> River over pebble, rock
> and sandy bar, a patterned
> language, a musical score—
> loss and longing in flux. If you
> stand middle of a causeway,
> your heart is a resonant chamber.

Sky like smoke appears in a deep saddle; cleared of trees the ridge carves a clean line. In a paddock to the left of the road, a loose-limbed and rough-barked apple stands in sharp relief to the billowing green that's a stretch of vintage oaks on the river's front. An imported gesture, a capitalised line planted last century, it's a different species of standing.

> A timber bridge so bowed
> it's a cello, and pavement so
> patched it drives like a riffle.
> I ford a shallow crossing; up
> ahead a Dodge Ram fishtails
> and bellows in a cloud of dust.

There are too many bridges on the river road to keep count. The current is on your right, and then it's on your left—so the rhythm goes. I arrive at Archinal's Bridge in a hurry, make a sharp left and then I'm on it. Its ragged beams are sound beneath my wheels.

New bridges of reinforced concrete and hot-dipped railings of steel have replaced some of the old spans. While wider than their forerunners, they're still one lane only. Perhaps it's economy, or a matter of heritage; I like to think that one lane means slowing, means giving way. Today I stop often, and walk the stream away from the road.

>Two magpies squabble, then sing
>   so I can cry. A bright blue wren
>and jenny work their dance moves
>   along a springy bough barely
>above the water. A brook,
>   the birds, and this unnamed crossing.

Halfway to the upper Allyn, the tarmac ends and the dirt begins. Now the crossings are low causeways that act as weirs, and the river washes your wheels like a saint—a moment of reflection for both driver and water. Once more I take a break from getting somewhere—from being someone—and walk in the shade of the rainforest which grows prosperous along the river's course.

>Flanged cedar stumps—notched
>   for standing boards—rot from the inside
>out. These are the half-masted
>   markers of a red cedar rush;
>you see them beneath the black-
>   hearted sassafras and supple-jack.

Come early afternoon I drive from the Allyn over a range of hills to the Paterson—the Yimmang[46]. The fire-trail I follow branches without warning, and with my eyes on the rutted road, it's difficult to keep track of where I've been, and where I'm going. On the upper reaches of the Paterson I crouch down by a small creek that falls, then pools before it joins the main current; a teardrop at full term in a shadowed gully. Water skimmers move on it as if on glass, and the rocks at its edge are clothed in lichen. I leave this cool and shaded tributary and follow the main current downstream. The sky is spotless.

> Not far from the foothills,
>   a languid reach. Here, a distant
> honky-tonk plays—plink, then,
>   plonk. Listen for each loosely
> metred lick, and love the river
>   as it falls toward extinction.

If memories are a river, we can't be certain when we dip into them, whether what rounds the bend will revive us like the cool splash of water on the inside of our wrist, or if we'll be swept away half-drowned. A massacre was perpetrated downstream of here in February 1827[47]. Few of the killings of the Aboriginal owners of the Hunter Valley are documented; acts of mass extermination are secrets held tight. These murders were born of the bottom line: twelve Wonnarua massacred at their campsite on the Paterson, and an uncounted number of people drowned in the attempt to escape the shooting. Back home after a day run through by rivers, I avoid thinking about the details of these killings by watching a cold case on Stan instead.

The squatter lives within us
      all, and that's why we lose our girl
and our boy. We're deaf while they cry
      "Stop hurting my beautiful
body!" He won't leave, he steals
      our sweet water; he pumps us dry.

To the River Again

The bank of the river is tight-knit stone pitched at a steep angle. It wears a cap of loose soil and offers few footholds, but I've made up my mind I won't stop until I stand by the water. I push on westward through the scrubby edge of the rainforest in search of a favourable slope. Several times I begin to make my way down, only to clamber back, feet and hands alive with the fear of a sheer fall.

I'm alone on this trip to the river. Before I set out, I configured my smartphone to send an SOS. Now all I have to do is push the on/off button four times in quick succession, confirm my intention, and a message is sent to family and friends; it tells them where and when. And yet, contemplating such a rescue makes me squirm, and brings me the patience to carefully unhitch my day pack from the teeth of a lawyer vine, who wants an improper fee for my passage. In the end, my descent is uneventful; by the water I look around.

> The river streaming, the forest;
>> Eden's here in a cool breeze.
> A dragonfly—ember-red
>> angel—dives to sip the river's
> rushing. If I could wing like
>> that, you know, I'd have my own show.

The upper reaches of the river are a gash through the forest. Sunlight finds its fractal selves on the current's broken surface, then it's gathered-light again, a slick on the curve of the water's falling.

> I'm not far above Blue Gum
>> Flat, balanced on a line of rock

that perturbs the river's flow.
  Water peels away from its point;
a movement that betters Bach—
  trailing lines and deepening eddies.

The buzz-saw cicadas, and the sound of the river travelling its bed, crowd in around me; the sky is both near and far. I put my feet in a pool chill as the Tops it falls from, and bare my legs to the January sun. Every other moment, a leaf drops from a tree and spins slowly to the lively water below, goes from an aerial-being to a coracle bucked by the stream. I'm observing a radical form of acceptance, and it's laughable how far away I am from such equanimity about my own fate. I am however, exultant to have come to the river, to have shed the articles of my daily living, to have quieted the estrangement I too often feel, even in the company of those I care for deeply. If the river demands payment for its ministrations, I've no idea what currency it deals in. Maybe standing bare-legged and grateful in the water will do as an IOU.

Dreaming Above Carrowbrook

A one-lane road rises into the Mt Royal Range and on the steep sections of waterlogged clay my vehicle slews about as the lugged tread of each tyre—and sometimes all of them at once—lose and find traction again. There's a lay by and camping area at Youngville, and I pull up beside the National Park signboard and map. The engine ticks loudly as it cools, and I stand back to admire the canvas of splattered mud that's the sides of my VW. It looks better this way.

> On slick roads the car in my hands
> snakes at the edge of control.
> But Crimson rosellas race
> like stunt planes, tilt at the boles
> of blackbutts. No sweat for them,
> they steer with a fluid motion.

Rosellas outrun me to the head of Pierre's Peak Trail. The fifth pair I've seen today; each time their two-tone colour scheme of brilliant blue and carmine-red is a jolt to the heart.

It's a short but stiff climb to the peak, and the humidity is high. Soon I'm bouncing off my rev-limit, a lack of fitness made more confronting by the script I filled this week for blood pressure medication. Out of breath I pause on a high point of an undulating ridge, on a pile of Olivine basalt boulders, and look straight down on the heads of rainforest. I can make out the music of the Carrowbrook, its high notes carried upward by the steep and narrow cleft that's its valley.

I'm up here on a Monday. I resisted dutifulness, and my reward is to smell the stream below, to feel the refreshment of still wild places, and that includes the ones within me.

> As a boy my church had nothing
>> in common with a dark brick
> building, sombre pews or hymn
>> board. I longed for the mud lark and
> dive-bombing plovers, who
>> chased me on my way to the willows.

For a time in the seventies, my family rented a house on the floodplain of Dumaresq Creek in a tableland university town. Today the brook below me, feels no further distant than the creek whose steep banks hid me and my brother, those mornings our mother was determined we'd go to Sunday school. I'd be beaten before I'd sit on a pressed metal chair in the church hall; I knew it sucked the life out of me—the smell of the place told me so.

> Sometimes, silent and barely
>> breathing in our hiding beneath
> the bank, we were close enough
>> to study the layers of alluvium
> before us: umber and gold.
>> Here, an earthiness fills the air.

How much deeper into this forested country will I drive? Whose permission might I need? Without an answer at hand, I give my mind over to the state of the road instead; it looks passable, so I carry on for a bit. Anyway, far as I can see the forest is tight to the trail, and a three-point turn would be unwise. As these things go, a few bends on a clearing in the forest presents itself. I park and leave my car.

These ranges rise steeply, their upthrust is a scarp that causes heavily laden clouds off the Tasman Sea to rise suddenly, they drop almost two metres of rain a year. The amount of rain that falls up here means the ground is soft underfoot, and the flooded gum in front of me is a pale and heavenly upwardness. I rock back on my heels and scan the forest. Like the psilocybin in magic mushrooms, which takes full effect without warning, all of what's manifest here insists upon itself as a single organism, and the space between each velvety trunk and the next is a portal on stillness. For a short time, I know myself as a being with roots, in the thrall of the collectedness of mind that forests are.

A slow accretion, thought by
        thought—made by a mind that's many.
I think of the first peoples,
        and I picture how they asked—
with studied inclusiveness—
        where do these intruders fit in?

In the tussocky grass of the clearing, I stumble across a broken set of springs that wear a thick coat of rust. My best guess is they once belonged to a truck, a timber-jinker that hauled logs destined to be made into bearers and joists down in the sawmills. Now I know what I'm looking for, I identify the rotted steel rails of a chassis, and balanced nearby on a rock outcrop, the steering rods and the idler arm that once directed this contraption along forest trails. Other details emerge where I saw nothing before; weathered-grey stumps like chess pieces mid-game are dotted across the forest floor. They testify to the ghosts of the men who cut hardwood here.

Axe-men smoke their ready-rubbed
        tobacco, lean on the giant

they've felled. Too quiet, they fall
    to lopping limbs. A net of roots
below—fibres from node to node—
    trees can hear one another's screams.

When I consider how this forest was clear-felled without regard for what it takes for such a complex community to establish itself—above and below ground—I'm convinced the trees would have me drop like a dead branch, and rot with the leaf litter at my feet. Dizzy, with a feeling of pressure in my head, I return to the car and stand in the vee made by the open driver's door. I'll shelter in my shiny capsule if I must, but for now I breathe deeply of the upland air, and keep my eyes on the trees. Weeks later, I read Richard Power's novel *The Overstory*[48] , and am struck by the words of one his characters, "...the world's outlands are everywhere, and trees like to toy with human thought like boys like to toy with beetles." I recalled the fear I felt in this forest.

As quickly as it arrived, my dread passes. Tentatively at first, then with a measured confidence, I step away from the car and back into the clearing walled by sheer trunks of gums. Now I'm aware that worms make passage beneath me, I can almost hear their blind burrowing, and the ground becomes less a stage for human drama and more of a living thing; this feels like a type of detachment, and yet, I feel it with every bit of me.

On the far side of the clearing, I narrowly miss stepping in a wombat scat; a short note dropped in a night of nimble-footed lumbering. King parrots fly over, a daylight flash who won't let me forget how they came and where they're going. But it's three yellow-tailed black cockatoos above the tree-tops who steal the show; they plumb the sky's bottomless blue, fathom its depth with each weighted stroke.

Their soundings say, "You, too, might come to know your own sweet time." If I'm hearing them right, then and only then, will I quieten the hurried man I am.

Wanderings 2

Ash Island and its wetlands are not far from my home. I take my bike there and ride fast on the flat dirt tracks to get some miles in my legs, then stop by a tidal creek to study it for life. Last week it was fingerling mullet swimming against the flood tide at the stream's mouth, but today, I sweep the sky—like one who worships Ra—for birds. Mostly I search for raptors, watch them in their low-level flight, jinking and dipping as if barely suspended and about to stall, or at height, where they beat the wind with scything cutbacks, work the face of a southerly swell that's about to barrel.

The sea eagle, a juvenile, is flummoxed by the magpie, and though the larger bird of the two, it's losing the fight. The magpie is strident, an unforgiving leader of the local neighbourhood watch. I've seen adult swamp harriers and sea eagles brush off such attacks—a nonchalant tilt of their wings, a few flicks and they soar away. But this young eagle is floundering, and giving up, goes to ground. The magpie has more to say, emboldened it follows. I'm surprised—even if my experience of watching birds on the island has taught me to reckon with the unexpected—how suddenly the scene shifts. The eagle's sibling drops out of the sun. My view is obscured by long grass in the field, but I can just make out the eagles, their heads bobbing up and down. I don't see the magpie again.

Afterwards the unblinking victors each sit on a fence post. It's easy for me to imagine their filial bond—hard for me not to wonder about their sense of things, and to what extent we're connected as sentient beings. They let me within ten metres then, flapping their wings heavily, peel away over the marshland. They leave a downy wake behind them.

The black swan keeps her head up.
　　Clear of me she begins to call
her babies. A plaintive high
　　　　pitched plea, it becomes urgent—
Are you there?—Are you there? And
　　　　she cranes to look under the oaks.

　　I spy a pair swans in a channel of open water; they're
crossing a swamp in their elegant evening wear and beaks of china-red.
At my first sighting of them last week, they were escorting six cygnets—
all of them a mottled brown on matte grey, and almost half the height
of their parents. Today there are five. A fox, or maybe a wedge-tailed
eagle. The bills of the remaining offspring will soon turn a tincture of
red, and their feathers matte black—an undercoat in preparation for
the lustrous sheen they'll wear as adults.

　　As I ride away—and put a wide swathe of swamp oak
between me and a necklace of wetland ponds—I hear what sounds like
chortling laughter. Birdsong to mark my departure, the celebrations I
hear when a harrier slides away to quarter[49] another water meadow.

Downwind of a body of water
　　set about with meadow, sun-
bleached reeds glint purple-grey. They bend
　　my way. Ibis break cover
with weary beats, and my heart
　　grows tired of being this human.

　　For a time during the pandemic and its lock downs, the
island was busy with people who came to exercise and roam—more
people than I've seen out here before. People tracking by, or through,
the salt marshes and wetlands that are the feeding grounds and

roosting places for migratory shorebirds. Listen to their names: Far-eastern Curlew, Sharp-tailed Sandpiper and Bar-tailed Godwits and, sometimes in passing, the Red Knot. They winter here to fatten up, then these prodigious travellers join the East Asian-Australian Flyway to Siberia, or Alaska, for their breeding grounds. Other birds, like the white-bellied sea eagles, know the river as home all year long.

The lives of birds in the riverside suburb around my home are even more precarious. The closest thing to a forest around here are the mature trees which grow unmolested along the margins of the rail line to the coal port, and a few established trees in backyards. There was an Argyle Apple that stood next door, a tree whose twisted and furrowed trunk wore a wide crown of jade-blue foliage; a commodious home for a pair of white-faced herons. Last September, the absentee landlord had this elder cut down, along with a Norfolk pine of mythic proportions in the same yard. When this giant lay on the ground, it looked like a whale on the deck of a factory ship waiting to be flensed. But before it got that bloody, I made one last attempt to stop the killing; I told the tree surgeon as he strapped on his climbing spikes, how a pair of magpies had a long lease on the penthouse at the top of the pine. It was the truth, but then I feared putting him off his game, that he'd fall, or lop a limb of his own.

When the pine was chopped and chipped, it remained standing in my mind's eye as a ghost against the western sky. The magpies farewelled their home by taking turns to pick over the mound of earth where the stump of the tree had been. They found pale fragments of flesh there, lifted them and let them drop. They kept up their ritual, singing sweet and low beneath their breath till evening. As for the herons, I learned later that they moved in down the street, chose a well-established camphor-laurel and built their nest—a makeshift clutch of sticks—in a low branch over the street. When I walk by, I see the birds shit on parked cars below; it won't be long before they're moved on again.

One night recently, after putting out the garbage, I turned and looked up to where the great pine had stood, and once more found it hard to believe an entity so grand could be reduced to sawdust and wood chips in a day and half. I paused a while in the company of the still youthful spotted gum by the back fence, bathed in the light of a full moon falling through the tree's spare crown, and waited for the ache to pass.

Epilogue

"In the face of a rational scientific approach to the land, which is more widely sanctioned, esoteric insights and speculations are frequently overshadowed, and what is lost is profound. The land is like poetry: it is inexplicably coherent, it is transcendent in its meaning, and it has the power to elevate a consideration of human life."
—Barry Lopez[50].

A mid-summer morning, a clear and almost still day on Ash Island, and I'm cycling along a track that follows the southern arm of the Hunter River. The moon will be full tonight, and a king-tide has inundated the mangrove that borders the river. At a glance the woodland swamp is a gloomy crowd knee-deep in muddy water, their mood unrelieved by sunlight dancing off shifting panes of water. The track I'm following—itself just above the water line—will carry me to the bridge over the mouth of Cobbans Creek, where last week I spotted the shadow of an estuary stingray—*Hemitrygon fluviorum*[51]—moving along the bottom with the tide's influx. Absorbed in my memory of the ray's languid motion, I'm startled when a white-breasted sea eagle breaks from the mangrove and swings down as if heavily laden across the track in front of me. A big bird, it wings with a deliberate beat, and holds to a low flight-path until I lose it behind a line of paper-barks in the east. When I arrive at the bridge over the creek, I find in the far distance the indistinct shape of a bird high in a dead tree. I know it's the eagle I'd seen earlier, it's the kind of knowing that defies rational explanation, when detail—like a spare line in a charcoal sketch—is an intimation of a coherence which feels utterly dependable. Everything about the vague imprint on the sky says it's the same bird. Jan Zwicky[52] writes of a way of thinking that, in addition to analysis, "...can travel by extra-logical connections of images, similarities in overtone and structure." This sighting is an example of what she's getting at.

Notwithstanding the fidelity of my first impressions of the bird, I'm soon second-guessing myself. So I ride south-east and then north as fast as the muddy and potholed dirt road will let me; I hope to confirm my earlier sighting. Three furious kilometres on, I dismount before an expanse of salt marsh, catch my breath and study the skyline. The eagle is penned in black on a washed-out sky, perched at the top of a dead swamp oak; the stoop of its shoulders, the down-turned head and hook of its beak easily identified. It seems a fated moment, or is this what resonance with a place feels like? It causes me to reflect on the other places I've visited in the Hunter River catchment, places that inspired the poems in this book, and how when I gave them all my attention—studied them—it seemed as if those places opened to me. Here's Jan Zwicky again—"Under certain conditions of attunement, a resonance-body is formed." What a marvellous suggestion, if we truly devote ourselves to a wild place—or to a person for that matter—allow ourselves to be vulnerable to their finer points and form as a whole, we might become a "resonance-body", and reverberate with that place, or person, just as the body of a musician who bows or plucks a cello, will tremble in sympathy with the frequencies of the instrument's wooden chamber and tightly wound strings.

The Hunter's catchment is the largest in New South Wales—so there's much of this many-armed organism I've not visited. Perhaps by way of consolation, when I've a mind for it and lay down with my eyes closed, I'm able to re-visit the riparian places I have been to. It could be, for instance, the upper Allyn, its shallow flow over pebbles lapping with a chuckle and a sob against its root-bound and moss-fringed margins, or else, it might be the slow turning, roiling underneath there that's the north arm of the Hunter off Ash Island. I feel it within me and, depending on what part of the river my whole-of-being turns to, it's possible to discern the differing qualities of each one's fluvial motion, its relationship to light, to air, to rocks and the sea. While my pen marked the page, made notes so I that might remember, my body, that is to say all of me—organs, muscle fibres and sinew—recorded that particular stretch of the Allyn as a sparkling undulation, a celebratory wave, and the north arm in all of its ripped muscularity.

My everyday world is more often than not a world away from these transcendent realities. I engage with social media, I'm hooked to the net, and I bend to my smartphone like most of us in this information age. I revel in, and depend on these habits, but when I've time for reflection, I fear them, and the growing reach of my "cyborg selves (part screen, part machine...[53])", because they school me in the substitution of simulated experience for the real. Slow-time spent with the river and the country around it, acts as an antidote to the creeping digitisation of everything; the river dances a fullness of being back into me, reminds me of my roots in the earth, and of what it is to be analogue, human and alive.

Notes

1. Beginnings as the title for the introduction was inspired by J.A Baker's "The Peregrine", Harper Collins, 2006.

2. Ash Island is technically no longer an island in its own right. In the mid-1960s the New South Wales state government decided to create an industrial lands scheme by filling the channels between Ash Island and a number of other estuary islands. They named the new island Kooragang. The country that was originally Ash Island, is now part of the Hunter Wetlands National Park, which supports 112 species of waterbirds and 45 species of migratory birds; the red-necked avocet and far-eastern curlew to name a few.

3. Paul is a pianist attuned to the music that's poetry. He has composed a series of tone poems for piano in response to the Ash Island haibun in this collection.

4. Matsuo Basho, "The Narrow Road to the Deep North", translated by Nobuyuki Yuasa, Penguin Classics, 1966.

5. Aldo Leopold, "A Sand County Almanac and Sketches Here and There", Oxford University Press Inc, 1949.

6. Gregory Orr, "A Primer for Poets & Readers of Poetry", W.W.Norton, 2018, 82.

7. Frederic Gros, "A Philosophy of Walking", Verso, 2015, 83.

8. Gaston Bachelard, "Water and Dreams: An Essay On the Imagination of Matter", trans. E.R. Farrell, Pegasus Foundation, 1983.

9. Barry Lopez, "Landscape and Narrative" from "Crossing Open Ground", Charles Scribner and Sons, 1988, 67.

10. John Burnside, "Strong Words" a chapter in "Strong Words: modern poets on modern poetry", edited by W.N.Herbert & Matthew Hollis, Bloodaxe Books 2000, 260.

11. Charles Foster, "Being Human: Adventures in Forty Thousand Years of Consciousness." Metropolitan Books, 2021.

12. Uncle Paul Gordon a Ngemba man who grew up around the Barwon River, has extensive knowledge of sacred sites along the east coast.

13. The Dreamtime is the period in which life was created according to Aboriginal culture. Dreaming is the word used to explain how life came to be, and it is the stories and beliefs behind creation. In the Dreamtime, the natural world—animals, trees, plants, hills, rocks, waterholes, rivers—were created by spiritual beings/ancestors. The stories of their creation are the basis of Aboriginal lore and culture. Online source, https://www.aboriginalcontemporary.com.au/pages/what-is-the-dreamtime-and-dreaming

14. Keats' Letter Journal letter of 1819, quoted by Philip Levine "My Lost Poets: A Life in Poetry," Knopf, 2018, 183.

15. Henry David Thoreau, "Walden" Everyman's Library, 1901, 115.

16. Seamus Heany, "Feelings into Words" in "Finder Keepers: Selected Prose 1971 – 2001", Faber & Faber, 2002, 19.

17. "On the Delta" from my first collection "Broken Ground" UWAP, 2018, 40.

18. Susan Cain, "Bittersweet: How Sorrow and Longing Make Us Whole", Crown Pub Inc, 2022

19. Buson, "The Essential Haiku", Ed. Robert Hass, Harper Collins, 1994,75.

20. Iain McGilchrist, "The Master and his Emissary: The Divided Brain and the Making of the Western World." Yale University Press, 2009, 117.

21. Seamus Heaney, "Crediting Poetry: The Nobel Lecture", Farrar Straus and Giroux, 1995, 30-31.

22. Aldo Leopold, "A Sand County Almanac and Sketches Here and There", Oxford University Press Inc, 1949, Forward, vii.

23. Mark Tredinnick, "The Land's Wild Music", Trinity University Press, 2005, 19-20.

24. Mark Tredinnick, "To sing, to say: A lyric ethics for coming into country", Griffith REVIEW no.80, May 2023.

25. John Berger, "Portraits: John Berger on Artists", Verso, 2015, 267-274.

26. John Burnside, "Strong Words" a chapter in "Strong Words: Modern Poets on Modern Poetry", edited by W.N.Herbert & Matthew Hollis, Bloodaxe Books 2000, 261.

27. Ash Island is roughly ten kilometres from the mouth of the Hunter River. In fact Ash Island is no longer an island in its own right, but the western end of Kooragang Island. The channel between the islands was filled as a part of the NSW state government's Industrial Lands Scheme in the mid-1960s.

28. Wanderer is the common name for the Monarch Butterfly, a beautiful North American who now frequents the east coast of Australia in the warmer months, and has since about 1871.

29. Hexham-grey mosquitoes are a particularly large breed that lives in the swamps and wetlands around Hexham and Ash Island.

30. Awabakal: first peoples whose country reaches from Wollombi in the west, to the Lower Hunter River near Newcastle and to the south around Lake Macquarie.

31. The indigenous name for the yam daisy is murnong.

32. Seamus Heaney, "Feelings into Words" in "Finder Keepers: Selected Prose 1971 – 2001", Faber & Faber, 2002, 19.

33. Gaston Bachelard, "Water and Dreams: An Essay On the Imagination of Matter", trans. E.R. Farrell, Pegasus Foundation, 1983, 188.

34. The steelworks fouled the river, the ground it stood on, and nearby wetlands; over 600,000 cubic metres of toxic sludge was dredged from the river bed by BHP in a delayed clean up. On site contamination with heavy metals and toxic aromatic hydrocarbons were dealt with by concrete capping, and constructing a 45metre deep containment wall which is intended to stop poisons seeping through the groundwater into the south arm of the Hunter River.

Online Sources: "River's toxic legacy", Newcastle Herald 31 Oct 2012, Ian Kirkwood and Safety Fears Over BHP's Toxic Sludge" ABC News online, 5 February, 2009.

35. Gaston Bachelard, "Water and Dreams: An Essay On the Imagination of Matter", trans. E.R. Farrell, Pegasus Foundation, 1983, 185.

36. Christopher Alexander from "A Timeless Way of Building", Oxford University Press, 1979.

37. Mary Oliver, "Wild Geese: from "Dream Work", Atlantic Monthly Press, 1986, 14.

38. After James Galvin's use of the term in the opening paragraph of "The Meadow", Henry Holt and company, 1992, 3.

39. After Barry Lopez in the chapter "The Shallows" from "River Notes", Andrews and McMeel, 1979, 44.

40. The Williams River ran through Woonarua and Worimi country, and was known as the Dorribang, online source, Wikipedia.

41. Frederic Gros, ibid, 148.

42. The rehabilitation of the islands wetland eco-systems has depended on the scientific illustrations and notes of Helena and Harriet Scott, sisters who lived on Ash Island in the 1840s and '50s. They produced many illustrations of plant life and animals they encountered on the island, and also furnished illustrations of butterflies and moths for their father Walter Scott's publication, "Australian Lepidoptera and their Transformations". The Scott family left the island in the 1860s, and the island was then cleared for dairy farming, effectively eradicating the complex eco-systems the Scott sisters were able to enjoy and record.

43. Leonard Koren's "Wabi-Sabi: Further Thoughts", Imperfect Publishing, 2015.

44. Barry Lopez's "Arctic Dreams", chapter 7, "Country of the Mind", Vintage Books, 2001, 260-261.

45. These indigenous names for places and animals on the lower reaches of the Hunter River are taken from "Rediscovering the

Coquun: Towards an environmental history of the Hunter River."
Address given at the River Forum 2000 at Wyndham Estate,
Hunter River, by Glenn Albrecht, online source.

46. Yimmang is the indigenous name for the Paterson River.

47. "Colonial Frontiers Massacres Australia 1780 to 1930, an online source, http://c21ch.newcastle.edu.au/colonialmassacres/detail.php?=625 a research team headed by Associate Professor Lyndall Ryan, Centre for 21st Century Humanities, University of Newcastle

48. Richard Powers, "The Overstory", Vintage, London, 2019, 165.

49. Quarter – a term that refers to a raptor ranging over an area while hunting.

50. Barry Lopez, "Arctic Dreams", Vintage Books, 2001, 247.

51. Loss of habitat makes this stingray a threatened species.

52. Jan Zwicky, Lyric Philosophy, Revised 2nd edition, 2011, 48.

53. Imani Perry, from the foreword to James Baldwin's "Nothing Personal", Beacon Press 2021, ix.

www.ingramcontent.com/pod-product-compliance
Lightning Source LLC
Chambersburg PA
CBHW031007090426
42737CB00008B/717